serpentine loop

Books

V6A: Writing from Vancouver's Downtown Eastside
(coedited with John Asfour), Arsenal Pulp Press

Voice to Voice: an Anthology of Music and Transformation, editor, Otter Press

The Stanza Project, editor, Otter Press

The Writers Caravan, editor, Otter Press

serpentine loop

poems by

Elee Kraljii Gardiner

anvil press | 2016

Anvil Press Publishers Inc.
P.O. Box 3008, Main Post Office
Vancouver, B.C. V6B 3X5 Canada
www.anvilpress.com

Library and Archives Canada Cataloguing in Publication

Kraljii Gardiner, Elee, 1970-, author
        Serpentine Loop / Elee Kraljii Gardiner.

Poems.
ISBN 978-1-77214-054-5 (paperback)

        I. Title.

PS8613.A743S47 2016   C811'.6   C2016-901182-8

Printed and bound in Canada
Edited for the press by angela rawlings
Book design by Derek von Essen
Cover photo by Joan Naviyuk Kane *Nunavut from 37,000 ft*
Represented in Canada by the Publishers Group Canada
Distributed by Raincoast Books

The publisher gratefully acknowledges the financial assistance of the Canada Council
for the Arts, the Canada Book Fund, and the Province of British Columbia through the
B.C. Arts Council and the Book Publishing Tax Credit.

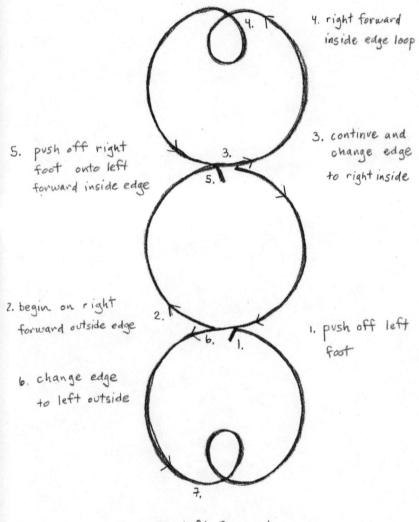

4. right forward
   inside edge loop

3. continue and
   change edge
   to right inside

5. push off right
   foot onto left
   forward inside edge

2. begin on right
   forward outside edge

1. push off left
   foot

6. change edge
   to left outside

7. left forward
   outside edge loop

Marking the Centre

SCRIBE

I was on the ice before I could walk.

In the womb then in her arms.

Seated in snowpants, I was the centre of an orbit she skated around me. Circular peekaboo.

The rink was a *de facto* living room where our family congregated and where I crawled, stood, raced, jumped, expressed myself and performed.

It was a family habit; my mother won Olympic silver ('52, Oslo) and gold ('56, Cortina D'Ampezzo) in figure skating for the U.S.

She was also a surgeon with little spare time; if she wanted to skate she took my two older sisters and me with her to The Skating Club of Boston.

On the ice I was treated like an athlete rather than a child. At the rink I recognized the first of many systems for ordering the world.

One of these systems was *compulsory* or *school figures*, a discipline that hones and demonstrates the skater's precision.

The skater carves predetermined patterns into the ice with the blade of one foot, re-inscribing the lines perfectly upon themselves three times.

up(on themselves
up)on themselves
up(on themselves

Although figures are no longer included in routine competitions, some skaters continue to practice them in 45-minute "patch" sessions, so-called because each person is assigned a patch of ice large enough to skate a figure eight.

I skated patch sessions a few times each week and loved the meditation of it even as I chafed against the stricture that figures demand.

Our rink had 22 patches. No one wanted the patches on the ends where the corners are rounded because the allotments are smaller. The patch at the Zamboni entrance was everyone's last choice, too.

While there is no gender division in figures—everyone skates the same patterns—the figure I equate with the technical mastery of my female role models is one I never managed before I left skating: the serpentine loop.

It's also one of the most pleasing, both as a pattern left on the ice and as pattern of movement in the body as it is performed.

Though the figure can take a moment to learn theoretically, it requires months or years to execute flawlessly.

The serpentine loop is a three-lobed figure that can be skated forwards or backwards.

To begin, the skater assesses the patch space, visually aligns the long axis and with the heel of her blade marks the centre of the figure—her point of departure and return.

She makes one and a half circles and a small ellipse on one foot, then pushes off on the other foot to mirror the shape on the bottom half of the figure.

She creates five shapes in total—three main lobes and two smaller ellipses at the ends.

The size of all school figures is determined rationally, mathematically, in relation to the skater's individual body. In a serpentine loop, the diameter of each large lobe is the skater's height. The diameter of the smaller ellipse is the length of her skate blade.

She learns to skate a figure by laying it out with a scribe, a tool that functions like a compass. It's an "L"-shaped telescopic metal tube with a handle on one end and a nail to scratch the ice on the other.

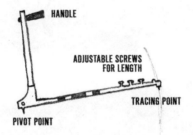

To practice, she skates on top of the circles etched by the scribe, tracing them over and over to learn the dimension of the figure and the surety of her line through muscle memory.

In my mother's time when the skater didn't have a scribe she would lie down on the ice to check the measurement.

The body becomes the measure becomes the line. The body written into the ice.

Our shared vocabulary ripples with possibilities. In poetry a twist of words raises the pulse. A smooth paragraph lulls the reader. In figures, a *paragraph* is a small two-lobed loop skated entirely without putting a foot down, using only the change of edge at the axis as momentum to bring around the body.[1]

Other loop figures use *three-turns* and *brackets*—moves that allow the skater to change direction much the way a poet turns the sense or argument of the sonnet using the *volta*.

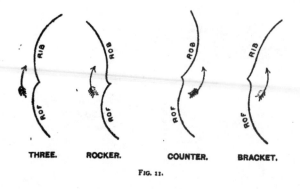

Fig. 11.

Examples of turns skated on one foot. ROF stands for Right Outside Forward, meaning it is skated on the right foot leaning on the right edge of the blade going forward; ROB—Right Outside Backward; RIB—Right Inside Backward.

The blade melts ice via friction and pressure.

I drifted away from skating but the language is imprinted in me. A tracing, a line extending beyond the margins.

---

1 Paragraph figures are traced six rather than three times.

Push Off

INSINU

The river sews itself into the city's muscle
with stories, admonishments against skating

alone at night: how our mother's friend, swallowed by water,
resurfaced. How, alone, he retraced the proven

circuitous route rather than risk a shortcut.
How his clothes froze stiff enough to crack a joke.

How one of our grandfathers saw his son fall
through ice delicate as meringue,

how the hole widened, its edges collapsing
as he tried to pull himself out.

How our other grandfather
            lost his son to the winter river
without knowing when or how.

Always around ice, we were trained
for emergency: how to drag a line

or use a belt, even a coat sleeve.
How to spread our weight wide.

We knew the outline, what adults could handle

before they turned away. Newspapers dredged the rest.

ONCE A MONTH

She focuses on my skates.
Grey as cygnets, mine lack elegance
but equip me for my habitat.
I know where the Zamboni lives,
when to get a toe-loop in on a crowded session,
how to kick ruts in the third bleacher
without getting caught. Not yet confined
by gender, I cross as often as I like
between the powdery heat of the women's
and the bitterness of the urinals in the men's.

Her skates wait by the sink—tan, buffed, punched out
over the ankle bone, the tongue chewed by the habit
of laces. Foam pad stuffed down each throat.
She brings a tin from the bottom drawer,
peels off its plastic baggie skin,
tips it to wet a stone with oil
until it darkens like a whale's eye.
She slides the stone along the flat of the blade
in circles like the loops she will trace
tomorrow morning at Earlybird.

On the ice she is another woman.

She seems to skate away from me
more often than she approaches.
It does not occur to me that at the rink
I may be a different girl.

To sharpen the blade, she holds
one boot upside down on her fist.
So do I, little shadow. The cry
of the stone is raw, the rasp

of a rough-throated heron.
I mimic how she checks
for nicks with the pass of a thumb pad.
A white line opens, floods red.
Cold water stuns the cut
and she is quick to bandage me.
Iron, blood, steel, stone:
the blade shines when she holds it level to her eye.

She repeats this procedure monthly.
Though I am a careful observer I am no closer
to performing it myself.
She wipes the blades of excess oil,
snuggles each gleam of steel into terrycloth covers
and nests them in the skate bag we share.

Each step is as familiar to me as her stroke
from one end of the rink to the other:

      three crossovers to round the corner—
      the susurration of her blades, a pulse.

Her movements speak another language—
one I will command, eventually.

My edges skim the surface, blades silent no matter
how hard I skate. I have seen girls develop,
make an invisible act audible.

      Ahead of me is the possibility of jumping
from girl to woman, water to ice.

OUTDOORS, THROUGH

i.

I crouch, look for fish below the ice.
Grown-ups tell me snapping turtles sleep in the
mud but I don't believe

they can hold their breath or beaks closed for a season.
Not to be down there and live again months later.

The lip of the ice is a border town where I am about to learn
it is a bad idea to be something you are not.

I am not a snapping turtle; there is a line,
an edge not safe to push.

I push it—sink three feet down until little blades slice mud.
Sweet water floods my snowsuit. Cold stuns

my lungs. Head above iceline, blinking, gawping,
I stretch my neck. This dip in the drink

ages me instantly: now I know what it is
to want to undo something, to uncrack the moment.

A blue-eyed man lifts me by my hood, carries me away
from his body without soaking himself.

Stripped and wrapped in a blanket in the backseat
I drowse. Baptism, chrysalis, rite of passage completed.

ii.

The skates are put to dry by the furnace
where the babysitter put the stillborn kittens.

I squeeze between the wall and the fire, where I am not supposed to be.
Yesterday our cat had kittens. Two did not move

or open their eyes and my mother was gone. The babysitter
wrapped them in a towel, told us to build a box with food, water.

We had many things to do while she slipped away.
She was vague about where the little bodies went.

With an iron tool I nudge open the drawer of the incinerator.
Mounds of feathery ash pool at my feet.
I will be in trouble for this mess.

The ash is soft as fur; I cannot help but touch it
both hopeful and afraid that something will catch
the attention of my fingertips.

Fine as baby's breath or silk, the ash furrows into my palms,
rims fingernails. I fish out unmelted bottle tops,
count the needle teeth. I sit one in each cap.

Carefully, I ferry them to my room. The babysitter doesn't
recognize this cunning flotilla lining my windowsill,
and because of that I am allowed to keep it.

LEARNING TO READ AND WRITE

My mother lifts stars, fruit and fish
from the surface of the ice
for me. Her skate blades
draw the world near
the boards. Her hands are still
above the ruffle of her skating
dress—she glides, reverses
in sharp movements without lifting
her foot, propelled by the pendulum
of her free leg.

See the star she has danced there?
Now she uses both blades
to carve a pair of parentheses
for a pineapple's plump body.
She locks her boots in a V and hops,
chopping the spiky plumes.

The fish begins like the pineapple.
She adds a tail, pinpoints an eye
with her toe-pick, then drops
away, rounds the rink and delights me
with a spray of snow from her blades.
Mittens to my hips, I mimic her,
skate to centre ice and spin until lost.

The contrail of my scratch
marks how far I travel, my lack
of skill. What should be a nest
of revolutions meanders across
the ice like a string of unclasped pearls,
a failure, until I recognize
the first four loops spell my name
and I have something to show.

*e third or fourth day the water drains off at the
ges, and a dry, beautifully easy-going surface is
t. There is, in fact, no such perfect ice for
ating purposes as hard black ice, slightly thawing
the surface, if it is strong enough and well swept.*

QUALITY OF ICE.

OUTDOORS, ICE

Ice varies very much in quality, but from what

Through an ice hole. Hidden from the
moonlight in the shadow of a bridge. The delayed
surfacing of the body was probably due to its being
pinned under an ice sheet. Monday's rainstorm melted
and disturbed enough ice so that downstream current and
wind brought it to its place of rest. Twenty Metropolitan
Police began probing the Charles River bottom and combing
the shorelines for the remains. Dragged for several weeks. The
discovery of a sheaf of correspondence between the missing
brother and a friend in Colorado, suggesting the possibility
of a secret visit. The hunt. National proportions. Brown
overcoat. Rowed on the varsity crew team. Studied
Sanskrit. Twenty-two. Departed from the Boston
home at 184 Beacon Street at 10 o'clock on the
evening of January 23, 1947. Children were
first to notice the body floating.

*excessively hard, and chips up under the skate
ade very readily, and often in quite large lumps.
e of this kind is very tiring to skate upon, and
es not yield such a fast travelling surface as
mewhat softer ice. Ice which forms upon shallow
ater is generally of inferior quality, but the reason
r this is not clear. Since shallow water freezes
er quickest, its ice bears soonest, and, not being*

are, or should be, kept comparatively quiescent. It is practically impossible to perform the kind of figures which are skated continuously with a quiescent unemployed leg. The problem, indeed, is to use the unemployed leg to its fullest advantage, swinging it freely and, if possible, gracefully, so as to assist the execution of the figure. With regard to the position of this leg, the reader should refer to the International Skating Union Rules of Correct Carriage and Movement, already quoted (p. 228). He should especially note that the toe is to be turned downwards and outwards, and the knee slightly bent. This—the usual, but not invariable—position of the unemployed foot is well shown in Plate V., which represents Herr Grenander just finishing a curve of inside edge forwards. Herr Grenander, who is by far the most graceful continuous skater I have hitherto seen, makes the most of this orthodox position of the unemployed leg and foot. He frequently also brings that foot, with the toe turned downwards and outwards, in front of the employed, with the happiest possible effect. I have already referred to this peculiarity of style on the part of Herr Grenander when skating continuous eights (see p. 234). In the same way,

ABSURD FIGURES

There is a club to join and I want in. It's a special group
and initiation is a rigmarole but they keep out
the miscellany—the one-footed beaks, the hooks and pig-ears,
the loops. I am reasonably sure that's not me. I work
the room, not bent at the hips but with my knees swinging fiercely.
I ignore the judges and their wolf whistles, avoid assistance,
however kindly offered. I let my arms hang down—
hands must never fly above hips—only poets do that.
I swing like I own the joint; I take up mental space.
That's what good girls *do*. Judges know confidence
is thinnest when the toe is turned inward as far as possible
so I get into first position. I tend to pull up short and worry
about feelings but tonight I will overreach. I don't want to be
an amateur forever. Entering this echelon, I won't carry the
unemployed leg in front. A lot of it is luck:
an upright carriage may be silk-lined or it may be a red
wheelbarrow. So much depends upon a look
cast over the wrong shoulder. I've weathered a succession of
destroyals, now it's time to find an edge. *Don't blow it*, I coach
myself, *this is your chance*. All members must take a turn
at the door. I tilt my head accordingly so I can
keep an eye on the line as I progress. Am I in? Did I make it?
It's like being in love—they say I'll just *know*.

AGE-ELIGIBLE

At a certain level, she's enough
for some Senior-Junior vice.

She is currently under 21, 19, 16
at least turned 13—new

and whole to the over-age man.
A perfect pair, this date allows the man
a silver season of eligibility.

She cannot compete with this level
of overlap. He's over her once
she has been under him.

RIVER RESCUE, 1849

Skaters practiced edges and lines
on the frozen Schuylkill

with yards of rope belted
around their waists.

Trained to rescue,
they earned

The Philadelphia Skating and Humane Society
its name, still in use today.

PIVOT

At centre ice, the public-school kids are more down than up. Along
the boards, a parade. Kool-Aid stains, tight jeans, hair beads, lip
fuzz, bodies shooting off in elastic dimensions—breast buds, biceps,
thunder thighs—none of them destined for success here. I won't get
much done due to choppy ice and the crowd. Can work on spins, leave
the kids their repetitive laps. I'm older, not just because I'm almost
out of high school, but because I know what I'm doing. Lacing up, I
smile into my shins at the big talk. There's always one, some kid who
owns it all.

Anthony, in faded Celtics tank top hanging past his knees, holds
court with girls. Watches me sideways. Rough townie voice, more
charm than he knows what to do with. He can't bear it. Turns to me.

You a real figure skater? You gonna teach me some tricks?

Bench to ice I learn he's 14, lives with his grandmother, when he sees
her. Listening is all it takes to make him mine. The girls all want him
to play chase but he's busy proving his *bona fides*: first time on skates
he can go backwards, doesn't need the barrier, *watch!* No one at home
told him to bring a sweatshirt or what to expect. He's just murdered
by the cold. 110 lbs of shivering self-promotion.

We head around once, twice. He imitates my waltz jumps. His
cousin laughs, calls him *pussy* when he falls. Anthony's polite, got the
deference Southie boys have for elders—won't answer back in front
of me but he'll pound Carlos. *Gunna wail on him outside if he doesn't
fucking quit it, pardon me.*

This kid's thin as licorice with southern Italy in his skin, palms
stung pink from slapping the ice, and too proud to admit how much it
hurts. Tucks hands into the cave of his armpits. Is fearless the way he
throws his body behind his ideas. Will show neither embarrassment
nor need; both mean defeat. *C'mon*, I tell him, *take the mittens.* No

complications, no *thanks* or *I'll give them back.* Anthony's ballsy, that's for sure. Knows the play of fear and pride too well for a kid his age but maybe it's just me, so soft everything looks hard.

His body language teaches me a few things about what he's learned of this world. He stretches his neck to keep my attention, herds me to the boards with the assertion of a guy three times his age. A future of moves working for him. The curl of his lip. Young Caesar, leading from the chin.

The thing is, he's telegraphing hope so I let him. His ankles sag like trolley wires but he's betting I'll notice something, take him to a grander place. He promises to be here next week and there is nothing more I believe than that he is going to be broken, by love if he's lucky, frustration if he's not. The edge of him honed until lethal, the blade turned against him, filleting soul from bone.

I want to find him warmly dressed next week but the school group doesn't come back. I take the ice, warming up with three turns, switch from outside to inside edge along the blue line, meander into swizzles and pivots, look at the score of the surface. The toe pick in the circle reminds me that self-sufficiency is a means not an end. It's likely I am the only one who will remember the boy's moves. I stamp against the cold, impatient as a racehorse while the Zamboni erases. The lost-and-found box holds a sad compost of Bruins jerseys, hats, balled socks, my old mittens turned in on themselves. He could have kept them.

Two Turns, Change, Two Turns.

ROF, RIB, ROF, RIF, ROB, RIF and LIF, LO
    LIF, LOF, LIB, LOF
LOF, LIB, LOF, LIF, LOB, LIF and RIF, RO
    RIF, ROF, RIB, ROF
ROB, RIF, ROB, RIB, ROF, RIB and LIB, LO
    LIB, LOB, LIF, LOB
LOB, LIF, LOB, LIB, LOF, LIB and RIB, RO
    RIB, ROB, RIF, ROB

Loop, Change, Loop.

ROF, RIF and LIF, LOF
LOF, LIF and RIF, ROF
ROB, RIB and LIB, LOB
LOB, LIB and RIB, ROB

Bracket, Change, Bracket.

ROF, RIB, ROB, RIF and LIF, LOB, LIB, LOF
LOF, LIB, LOB, LIF and RIF, ROB, RIB, ROF
ROB, RIF, ROF, RIB and LIB, LOF, LIF, LOB
LOB, LIF, LOF, LIB and RIB, ROF, RIF, ROB

TRESPASS

i.

The diggers come to harvest
at low tide. Worms for cash.
They arrive in bumperless hatchbacks.
They park by our pastures,
keep their heads down
like children who know not to press their luck.
They hold pails and horror-story rakes.

I hear the rough guffaws
before I see the men from the deck
and I hope they will be quiet,
dull their commotion
so as not to draw the attention
of the adults who are sunk in reading.

We do not speak
to the worm-diggers,
whose livelihood depends
on transgression and trespass
across private land.
We allow them access but it's a tolerance,
an inherited pact of silence
like the tide, another quiet force.

ii.

A couple of words, a stretch
of vowels broad as their chests
so unlike our own
then silence as they breach
the path near the house.
I must not meet their faces;
Grandmother insists familiarity breeds
complications. My eyes touch
their muscular backs. Those legs
as if in seven-league boots
make quick work over the fallen pines.

These men—only ever men—move
as ruined athletes. In single file
they jump from rocks to mud
into the world beneath their feet.
No one looks up at me
behind the wrought iron railing thick as my wrist.

The diggers are another coastline
treacherous as the poison ivy, sumac and oak
that keep me out of the woods. Their menace
is never proven. Their work spurs a bruise
of pity from the adults. Grandmother casts an eye
at the mudflats, swirls gin against the rocks
of ice in her goblet. She changes
the subject when I ask.

So we decided to leave the endless trail and stop pretending we were mountain men because we weren't. At the bottom of Chairback Mountain, four miles farther on, there was a dirt logging road. We didn't know where it went other than that it must go somewhere. An arrow on the edge of my map pointed south to Katahdin Iron Works, site of an improbable nine-teenth-century factory in the woods and now a state historical monument. According to my Trail Guide there was public park-ing at the old iron works, so there must be a road out. At the bottom of the mountain, we watered up at a brook that ran past, and then started off along the logging road. We hadn't been walking more than three or four minutes when there was a noise in the near distance. We turned to see a cloud of dust heading our way led by an ancient pickup truck moving at great speed. As it approached I instinctively put my thumb out, and to my astonishment it stopped about fifty feet past us.

We ran up to the driver's window. There were two guys in the cab, both in hardhats and dirty from work — loggers obviously.

"Where you going?" asked the driver.

"Anywhere," I said. "Anywhere but here."

I'd better go back up.' But suddenly there's a *lot* of uphills, and a lot of downhills too, and it's real confusing. So I went up and up and up until I *knew* I'd gone a lot farther than I'd come, and then I thought, 'Well, Stephen, you stupid piece of shit' — 'cause I was getting a little cross with myself by this time, to tell you the truth — I thought, 'you must have gone too far, you jackass,' so I want back down a ways, and *that* didn't work, so then I tried going sideways for a while and — well, you get the picture."

"You should never leave the trail, Stephen."

"Oh, now there's a timely piece of advice, Bryson. Thank you so much. That's like telling somebody who's died in crash, 'Drive safely now.'"

"Sorry."

"Forget it. I think maybe I'm still a little, you know, unsettled. I thought I was done for. Lost, no water — and you with the chocolate chip cookies."

"So how did you get back to the trail?"

"It was a miracle, I swear to God. Just when I was about to lie down and give myself to the wolves and bobcats, I look up and there's a white blaze on a tree and I look down and I'm *standing* on the AT. At the mudslick, as a matter of fact. I sat down and had three smokes one after the other, just to calm myself down, and then I thought, 'Shit, I bet Bryson's walked by here while I've been blundering around in the woods, and he'll never come back because he's already checked this section of trail.' And then I began to worry that I never would see you again. So I really *was* glad when you turned up. To tell you the truth, I've never been so glad to see another person in my whole life, and that includes some naked women."

There was something in his look.

"You want to go home?" I asked.

He thought for a moment. "Yeah. I do."

"Me, too."

vii.

Their laughter pulls. I linger, ripping
handfuls of sweet grass for the stallion,
stealing looks when one pulls his suspenders
off, his orange T-shirt written with sweat.
Up close they are taller
than my father and have codes
I don't understand.
The man in orange swings his bucket down and I risk
an offer I hope the stablehands won't betray.
The stubble on his chin shines golden
red in the afternoon sun.
He brings me closer with a jerk of his chin.
I meet his eyes, which are lined with wrinkles
precisely the shape of the rake hanging by his knee.
I blush, cut away, look at my feet.

He tips the bucket to show me
sloshing water that breaches the lip.
A swirl of convulsions, each worm thick
as my thumb, long as my ponytail.
Lunging things with teeth staggered
in circular, cannibalistic mouths.
He shows bite marks on his hands,
a buffet of recent and faded scars
the colour of Shiraz my father prefers.
My stomach heaves at the tally.
I say *the salt must sting*,
which sets his buddies laughing.
He lobs a joke I don't get.
Go on, he says, confusing me
with the invitation of his smile.
I invent a chore and refuse
to come out of the barn
until the hatchbacks have cleared off.
Only later, alone between tides, I walk
down the middle of the road as if I own it.

Change of Edge

FALLING THROUGH

The uncle I never met skated
up the river one night, maybe after a fight with his mother.

Tired of the slaughter of gin bottles by the piano
maybe she wanted him to get serious,

buckle down, grow out of unnatural attachments to his pals.
Make a bid for a girl. I imagine

the banks of the Charles were white as Noël Coward's scarf
and his cheeks ignited with pleasure of exerting the right

to live as his own man, maybe with a man. These are suppositions.
But they say my uncle Sylvester, golden enough to be called Silver,

had a sweet touch, an easy way, a charm of dimples.
His sister remembers he was too sensitive. He had perfect pitch.

If I were a boy I was to be named for him.
He was not the first Sylvester in the family to drown.

RENDER

Hunt and harpoon, survive:
stay away from home port until winter ice breaks.
I return to harbour loaded down with an idea
so large I carve steps in the carcass to mount it.
The compulsion to examine vessel by vessel
this massive muscle, to alter the shape
of what outweighs me with implausible numbers, tears.

The hull of a Blue is tendered starboardside,
fins tucked prim to the wood of my ship.
A handsome blade ready in my fist.
I slice a ladder into—and of—the flesh
dressed in oil and seawater, blood and wine.
        Butchering's a lonely alchemy.

Tick off: *Baleen, Sperm, Blue, Gray, Right,*
recite taxonomy to keep me
bobbing safe above the slaughter. My lungs are packed
with guitars and seagrass, bonfires, vital information
inked in a violet common to mussel shells.

        I contain neither feeling nor language.

Crawling up the slope
heaving aside hunks of what is missing
I find the pulse I have laboured to put out. Still,
I render archives of solitude in the try-pots,
liquefy flesh, barrel and label the material.

Away in oily smoke goes the mammoth.

My wrists are stained, hope's slick dressing coats my skin.

Reduced, I pace the length of the ship
to spell the tonnage of absence in footsteps
that leave no trace on this wet deck.
        On the horizon is another, I believe.

Yet the heart, like the orphan calf,
is a dory circling what it knows of belonging,
keening at the crisp distance between bodies.

TERRITORY

First our Christmas kitten disappears,
then a neighbour's longhair is swiped
cleaning her paws by the koi pond.

I open the gate one morning
and interrupt a deuce of coyote
scouting the street. Scruff grey,
lanky and humourless, the larger sears me
with a glance, puts me in my place.

Fear invades the riding.

Petitions for a cull materialize
and I delete them. Spin *samizdat* theories
of my own on territory,
how it belongs to the larger brute.

Schooled not to play by the shrubs,
the children spend recess indoors memorizing
silhouettes: one of dog, one coyote.

What, I wonder, are the coyote pups being taught?

At home
my daughter tells me I did it wrong that morning.

> *Make yourself big, you have to*
> *stare it down,*

she says through gulps of juice.

> *We are too big already,* I say.

I flip the paper to hide
         photos of a car bombing.

Then early before light rebuilds the known world
I slip to the window to witness
         one sitting sentinel
at the curb as its partner in the bushes
                    rouses a meal, herds it to the jaw.

Word has it
down on Musqueam Reserve
Animal Control shot one,
tracked it
bloody along the golf course
to a den
littered with 167 pet collars.

I know this, I tell my neighbours, *I saw the body
loaded in a van that day I walked the banks.*

It was taken to an office
where procedure calls for carcasses
to be weighed, measured.
I heard the uniformed hunters praise
the corpse, largest in memory, as I scraped
mud from soles and the Fraser River
         continued its constant intrusion into the bay.

BOUNDARY FOR THE MARRIED

Approach an electric fence with caution—
a blade of sweet grass extended
between thumb and forefinger. Lay the tip
of green upon the wire: it dances

when the line is hot. Forget about touching metal
with bare hands, closing the circuit with your body.
Register the thrum of this green blade as pleasurable
warning. Every so often a heartbeat will gallop loose

and threaten the collusion of crickets,
the patience of funnel spiders. Commotion,
while electrifying, is short-lived and for better or worse
we do not forget. The bite of the wire on an open palm

will remind you your job is to stay clear, to respect
the divide. How long you carry the imprint depends
on the intensity of the charge and your impulse to stay.

SPIRAL

Charlotte, I can piece it together.
Your man, deployed and returned,
perforated by the names of privates
and some one-syllable southerner
whose body swirled like confetti
leaving nothing to send home.

He's split into before and after.
Unable to follow through on anything
but a punch. Maybe you connect, maybe you dodge
his questions by degrees. It's not my job to watch
for the gun by the bed, the Colt in the car,
the pipe in his hand replacing your name. So what
if the T.V. is on when he's home, always on.

I'm interested in how I make your pulse race,
not the dates of his tour, that he's living
in a country of downers, pot and pain.
My gig is to make you forget the desert, abandon
the wait. You want to extinguish the wedding votive,
lose the loop of violence? I can loosen the yoke.

I am a nowhere man, built for take-off,
nothing to leave. He's the soldier, but I know exit wounds
depend upon level of contact.
Whether you pack it in or he re-ups,
don't turn to me then. Configure whatever
borders will hold you together. I'll be gone, traceless.

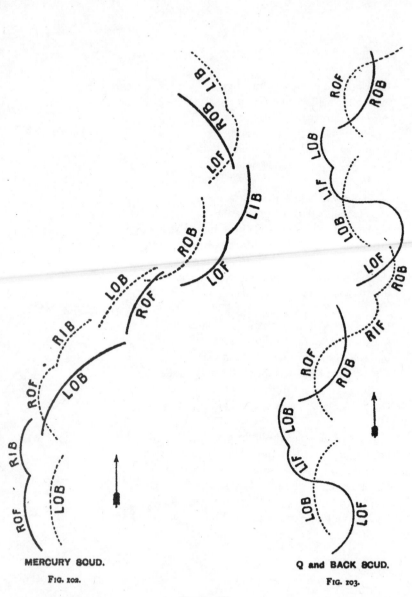

MERCURY SCUD.

Fig. 102.

Q and BACK SCUD.

Fig. 103.

PLATE IX.

[*To face p. 271.*]

MERCURY SCUD

Husband, you led me to believe we would travel hand in hand
albeit through cloudy days, to *future* and *family.*
While I was distracted folding silver into laundry
you set little missiles to explode without warning. In a snatch
something violent, angular and stiff skated across your face.
I measured the mercury, lived by degrees under an expert
who knew how to apply tactics. You kept cruel
forces dispersed and hidden, coming by it honestly
apprenticed to parents whose fury travelled faster than sound.
Your emotions ran like clouds scudding across the sky.
Slap, beat, spank: the effect was psychological
as well as physical; I scattered. I couldn't catalogue
your many species of violence so I focused on what moves fast
in a straight line. Fact: scuds are tiny relatives of crayfish, water
fleas and shrimp. They live in streams, ponds and lakes, bodies
that appear to be attractive from a distance but are, in fact,
unattractive when viewed closely. *Like you*, you laughed.
Truth: I don't like shallow water. I am female, but a female—
I mean, a *woman*—with a face rarely found in rivers.
Your explosions had devastating consequences
but here's a fact: a scud is also a scab on a wound.
When I got away I had to remind myself another kind of scud
is a flight of larks.

> And it would never occur to you
> > to pierce the clouds,
> > > look for me above.

WHO YOU ARE BY WHAT YOU RECOGNIZE

angel   battle rattle   blue line   boards
bombaconda   bye   camel   chack/chacked/chacking
cheated   check   cherry flip   choke   CHUville
clean program   coalition county   code of points
combination   compulsory dance   compulsory figures
counter-turn   cross stroke   crossed step behind
crossovers   crouch   death blossom   death spiral
dirt sailor   discipline   double   draw   edge
edge jump   element   envelope system   exhibition
extension   fan spiral   figures   fixed wing   flight
flood   flutz   fobbit   four continents   frago
Frankenstein   free leg   grade of execution   grapevines
green zone   haircutter   hillbilly armor   hollow
hop   hydrant lift   I-spin   inside edge   inside the
wire   jingle man   jingle trucks   jump sequence
kiss and cry   landing leg   layback spin   leg wrap
lift   lip   lobe   local nationals   long program
lunge   mohawk turn   mortaritaville   nationals
open stroke   operation enduring freedom   ordinal
outside the wire   over-rotated   pivot   popping
positional jump   presentation   professional   quad
red on red   red zone   REMFland—*more a state of mind than*
a physical location—   Rittberger   rocker turn   roll
Russian split   sanction   sandbox   sandpit   sasha
spiral   scratch   senior level   shake and bake   sheep
jump   shoot-the-duck   shotgun spin   side by side
signature move   Soldatova rule   spread eagle   stag
step-out   stroking   sustainer theatre   swizzle
synchro
'Tano jump   technical controller   throw jump
traveling   wet chu   Y-spiral

COSTUME MAKER, 1960

I work a secret language, sew into his seams
a costumed language of rick-rack, plackets, pin tucks, gussets,
patterns that I dream as I sit plotting.
Intention feeds through the sewing machine.
I dress my husband for the tours,
see him feed on crowds and pose, lift a pen,
smile bright, arm light upon the shoulders of his fans.
I'm tied tight to his caprices as sequin stitched to epaulet.
He depends on me, asks *if* and *should*,
believes I hold his interest dear, though

some things are not spoken of—
his fist shears off what I'm allowed: a shadow-life
behind his curtain. I fade like house lights
when he's on. Pacific moon, I can't eclipse
the star. Once, I sparkled in another's eye
then read the lesson in purple and in blue.
Bruise turned yellow, I turned quiet

but my fingers run freely through yards
and bolts. He does not recognize
the cleverness or care about the messages
along the knife pleat. Prick stitch, bar tack, whip stitch,
flat-felled seams, pattern weights, roll lines,
released darts—my needle speaks for me.
Pressed against his skin the drape of a different story,
basted and reinforced, stitches even and clean.
Each pierce I aim with violence; I am not what he sees.
I bide the time, align the pins, choreograph the scissors'
whisper by upthrust chin too quick for him to scream.

ICE IS THINNEST UNDER A BRIDGE

i.

World War II summoned Silver's father and brothers to accolades, to medals.
His sister shipped to Nevada, read novels in solitude while test bombs exploded

behind her desert hut. Silver's plans were on ice;
he was too young. He dressed just as the war collapsed upon itself.

His first and only month in uniform he opened the doors of a camp
for prisoners fed on shadows. He stayed in such dark rooms

although his safe homecoming was trumpeted.
They said heroism, he said nothing.

He emptied his memories into bottles of spirits.
Turned up the volume to arrest the flow of images

through the barracks of memory, a private
torture when the music stopped. The burden forced him down

like a headmaster's firm hands on his shoulders
keeping him pinned to his seat until chapel finished.

Did he have time for sound? I think of the end of his forward propulsion,
his body anchored by instruments of escape, floating under—

the spasm of his lungs in that sharp water, tighter
than a bear hug from his father, the Governor. The trap of laces.

The current sweeping him downriver. Swim strokes under a surface capped
with ice. Red ribbons made of his legs, a castaway's tatters.

The thaw produced what his roommates could not: his body, the end
of its slow-as-the-blues journey to the mouth of the Charles basin by his
mother's door.

ii.

Interpretation is a fluid record; we read the surface through steel,
through spine and devise a silvered history of how
we treat each other. Sliver of chance

we are accidents, happenstance, just shattered
film crystallized in partials: the purr of a snowsuit
zipper, the run of fingers up the scales.

While one is treated like a hero for surviving,
another is damaged by survival. The river bleeds out.

We rarely test the milkwhite under the inch.
We are always in the act of falling through.

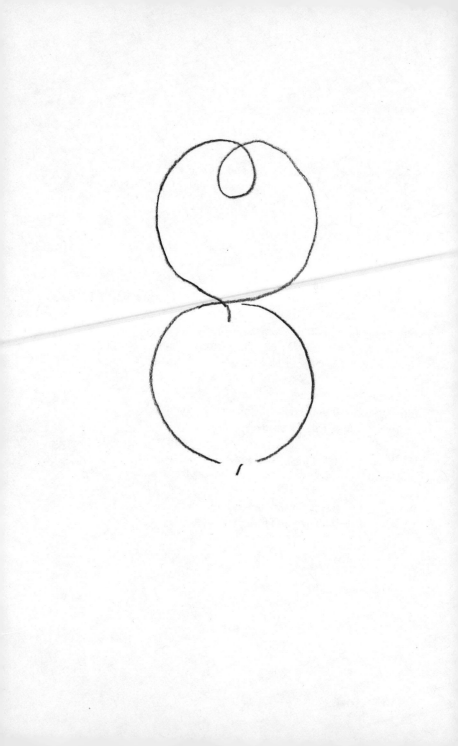

SUPERSEDURE

swarm hangs
      from the lilac
            drips
                 onto the lawn;

                  a living pool

      drones do not question
           workers attend
    her, drones fumble to mate, thwart her
     efforts
           to navigate,

a colony
      lifts up
                                     r i s e s

          in me, an affinity for the queen

restless, incensed

(who thrives, whose
humdrum insistence?)

someone always   follows

chattering

endearments

who can remember

to revel, slow, soften like wax?

am separating

colours from whites, child from child

fat from bone

am blocks away

in the blackberry bushes

nectar-drunk and rolling in an exorbitance of pollen

the youngest child learns

to use my first name

if he wants to turn my head

in the eaves
           a muscle of wax and honey

ninety-pound nest swollen
           chugging with bodies

               luscious vibration removal

             ladder: suit: smoke-out:

hungover workers, entourage

                    thousands of gluttonous stunned

bodyguards

          to obey the short-lived directive

            save the queen

(where is the queen?)

throng congregates midair

     and streams into
               tiny
           opening

of new home

     as if they never meant to leave

vacation, an idyll, some folly

docile clusters inside (where is the queen?)

     we chisel off

         chunks

   fat as pumpkins

            candle scent on concrete lasts until next rain

air-travelling bodies:

hive to river : river to hive : hive to river : river to hive

queen is failing

to fatten up

on the sweetness of home

a cuddle

death
looms

colony purrs
        searching for queen's scent (who is the queen?)

        drone schedule of pickups
      such lulling sedation spiked by private terror:

               supersedure

          begins with the gesture of enfolding

hive cloisters, heating, smothering

the urge to replicate, rebuild
is profoundly cell-based
        private decisions yield symmetrical decision

       hive-structure cools then ignites
the message of nectar in the matrix:

                  protect the dweller, protect
                  the dweller

AUBADE

My colour rises
        and the garden exhales

~ *petit mort* ~

Tonight the bloodroot petals shock, drop.

        Purple Winecup tightens
        against chill malignancy closing shut,
        shut.

Inside the calyx of the breast, blight takes hold:

                  cell
        atypical | division: : ;

I put the garden to sleep.
Prune back fear.
Slice stem from stalk, repeat
until a skeleton emerges.

Protocol is three weeks on, two weeks off.

Waiting in the outpatient lounge I question
how much of me is frost-hardy. I am

                trained to

                a stake.

                Slow

                drip

                of

                pesticide.

                                The nurse wears gloves.

I become the rose bloom of blood in needle.
Become plum colour swelling at joints.
Preyed upon by butterfly clamps, I flutter,
brush at mustard stamen stains under my eyes.

Bruised by scent of Naugahyde and disinfectant
I am isolated, one stalk in sterile vase.
Wrapped in plastic.

      First frost. Birdcall absent. Thrush veins the late hours.
      This night has lasted months.

The inside of my forearm is written with winter ivy.

Doctors lattice me to a painful agenda of guesswork.
Opportunistic parasites take hold; statistics plant me
at the gravesite, a *Lisianthius nigrescens*.

Dormant, I sip colour,
borrow belief from the Stormy Weather,
her smoky purple bloom and deep green foliage
chosen for disease resistance.

    I'm canny; I quiet crocus.
     I seek root systems,
   cleave to the rhythm and cycle
of the ice machine.

        Lean towards windows
         where I sense a quiver in hue,
a slight thrum from the east. *Aurora*
bleeding heart, Silene stenophylla.

    Revival smells of darkness, not loam
    but something scarcer.

I fever through the swailing
    while they monitor the brush fire.
They count the snap of cones and seeds,
interpret any augury with percentages.
    They maintain
    they expect the body to germinate.

Streams of killer language flow over, not into me. I husk.
    Accept a sip: a cup: a glass: this litre, drained
until one softened spot breeches with green.

Now half-formed and raw, dedicated
to the practice of revival

      here I am spring-loaded with pollen.

DOPPELGÄNGER

My grandfather smokes in the hospital
(they all do), none realizing
ash and nicotine violate the Hippocratic oath.

Miss Fredericks, his nurse, presses
his palm with instruments crafted in Europe.
The heft of that icy metal slices through
subcutaneous layers like a hymn.

In the medical school photo he stands
beside a man butterflied and propped
as if struggling to rise,
skin peeled from muscle and tendon,

the cranium sawed and hinged upwards
at an angle such that the dead man looks
to be doffing his cap. A flirt, a cad.

My grandfather beams a hero's smile
formaldehyde dripping from his elbows.

Lunchtime: the repetitive prayer of hands to mouth.

The smell sticks no matter how much I scrub.

Others name the dead man Oscar so he will have a name.
Calluses on the palms and the ripple of muscle under skin
suggest that he, dead at 43, was a hard worker.
At other tables students struggle
with idiopathic structures and deviations.

By end of semester the trio identifies cherry

red spots in Oscar's grey matter, and determines
he died of carbon monoxide poisoning.

Every organ but this one lush, robust and sound.

At night my grandfather stacks medical
journals to the left of his bed. By morning
the pile stands on the right.

I press him to tell me why he doesn't
sleep while the world is still. He says he
thinks of Oscar then, of all the Oscars
and the difference one man might make.

MAIN ARTERY ALONG THE RIVER

Glass splinters.
Begin what you hope
will become this driver's story to tell.
Reach for gloves stocked in the dash.
Pull to the shoulder.
Touch the body you don't want to touch.
Bear down on the heart, swallow the gag that rises
when he vomits into your mouth.
Ignore everything but the saving of life.

Major blockage in his windpipe and the angle is bad.
Stem the flow. When paramedics arrive, feed them stats, vitals.
Assist. Carry his last whisky stains on your shirt.

Leave the E.R. without a name, bound by tensile lines
to the man bleeding out on the gurney.

For days the sensation of his open mouth turns you
off food. Eat out of duty.
The wounded take all forms.

STILL LIFE

The rain line drips at the alley's mouth
two figures against the wall
curl their shoulders
this is all it takes
to conjure a curtain of privacy
despite cars fuming a yard away
he unlaces her boot
baring a luminous ankle
taper of her foot
he raises his hand
to the light
twirls his wrist
raindrop, glint
of the hungry eye
she turns her face
to the neon, sweet
blue light catches scabs
and bruises on her face
the leg of her jeans
is slack with soak
laces drawl
she thrusts her foot forward
urgent for kiss of syringe
the rain strikes with little fingers
need glitters here
when he is brusque with the belt
it's because she is beyond
the bricks and he has a habit
of chasing her

RAISING A GIRL

I shove icicles into the bag,
pitch pricks and knives into
       the gappy sleeve of memory. *Watch out,*
I shriek to the kid.
          Too late—shards of ardour splice
a pink heel. My sloppy heart
sloshes in the pail. I recover. So does the child;
      she barely notices. This is my scar
      transposed to her skin; she must mark her own.

I prod the bank with a dull shovel,
uncover kisses, exchanges of danger.

      She makes a snowpanted discovery
      of a wagon rusted with salt crust.

              Crisp icicles
             spot the lines.
              Spines
               drip.

Hand in hand, I tell her
spring tends to dissolve
      the danger, mostly.
She is distracted, discovering her own conclusions.

      Up in the birch a bird's tongue
saws at silence.

She is blind to slag creeping
      under silent snow. I see
      a dark crust everywhere. She sees
patient white soft side.

My hindsight view is melt-smear;
bags of ice, stacked slump, slide into
predictable messes.

Some puddle.

She trusts certain forms, licks wagon metal,
sticks her tongue, melts salt.

The first flavor incises.

As mother I mustn't talk away the burn.
Words won't last as much as sear-scar.

The bird-tongue spit turning on
the slender spine of tree is not mine.

She pricks her ears to the sizzlewhistle of snow slide.
Birch curves to snow kiss, snow kill, snow line.

Relief: yes, she smells danger
notices ice-burnt switches.

) Mothering is crystalline (sometimes.

Glass-crusted birch drips a final sizzle
and—crack!—the sting of spring strikes hot.

We are split, sunned, tremble with green,
she for the first, and how
many more.

Tracings

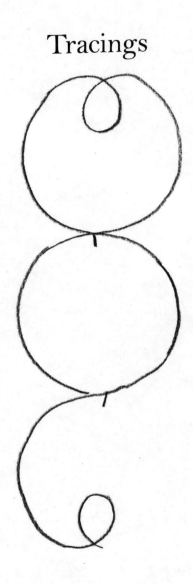

CIRCLE

After Robert Kroetsch

Inside you are the same: different ideas,
contagions as last winter/summer.
The rain is sharpening
into icicles. Sometime soon
spring will betray again
in different ways.
Punctuate the schedule
with fists and pump
proud ideals in the parking lot,
running towards the other guy
in anger. Struggle into his embrace,
grapple with the physical
sameness of anger/love.
This looping of humanness—

       we only have X amount
       of emotions to choose from;

we have already told all our stories.

OH, VANCOUVER

The city is one big in-law suite,
crowded by natural beauty,
        and lonely.

My friend feels bad about being depressed.

A woman I met
sends me one line:
        I'm lonely.
Statuesque, articulate,
she is the city, yet also the forest
bruised by developments.

Hear us tapping on the stucco
too afraid of direct contact.

WORK OF RAIN

The beach whispers,
the truth of this city is in the grey.

We live within
a skirt pleated
by the work of rain. Wet hems
us, becomes familiar
as mother's footsteps.

To survive here

is to navigate a water-pruned cartography.
We arrive at destinations flattened
by run-off, tell ourselves, *it's not so bad.*
Redirect seasonal affective disorder,
gloat. Think we are not so far
from nature, point to forest paths
carved by paws and hooves, parks
exhaling whorls of runners, multimillion-
dollar structures cantilevered
on cliffs mined with otter slides.

In the empty house a microwave pings, the only
company in a cold afternoon. Sleep
precludes dreams. We return to bed, joyless,
to sheets crushed with damp
sadness, a routine velour.

Downtown, corridors rush in plumb lines
to foreign markets and conglomerates.

A few blocks east, alleys collect footprints.

The map forms as we use it, etched
by the flow—not of water,
but what we do to each other.

Long lines circle the church;
tributaries winnow to
nothing.
Chainlink.
Behind the dumpster,
the surprise of human life
and what it can weather.

What do I know of loneliness?

Gulls gather in the rain. Together
they alight, flock and wait on the diamond
for a man and his bread. Come,
watch his hand glimmer while
he casts a fortune of crumbs.

      Ask me what I can trust so much
      as his defiant act of communion.

SCHOOL FIGURES

Cast in blue, grey and violet inside the hangar-sized rink,
we move to assigned patches, drape sweaters
on the boards. Place skateguards upside down.
Tiny hulls. Each of us is alone
with something to do: trace infinity.
Perfect the line we know dissolves under water and steam.
In the chill, we do not move quickly enough to sweat.
We round the figure like an unwinding clock,
push off and peter out; repeat three times. A coach
in a shin-length parka traces a girl, corrects her free leg.
Twenty skaters concentrate on line, repeat figures
until motion and time translate for body. A scribe
telescopes to the tape marking the skater's height.
The scribe's pivot and scrape is so familiar
it evaporates unheard, a breath.

OUTDOORS, WATER

On a warm beach littered with death, spines and urchins,
soft bodies float to shore beaten by the metronome of waves.

I nudge a Man o' War that shows no sign of life. Scores of them
slump, tentacles draped through sand like hair of the forgotten.

Each blister is an empty mouth, a lost chance to communicate.
I know enough to step carefully: even the dead can bite.

STEALING ANATOMIES

In this slow time the physics of terror
is simple as a window. She is naked
when men push her through.
Hair streams upwards,
her cry ricochets down brick walls.
Twisting: silk over alley.
Shadows engrave her nude back,
blades of light scale her skin.

The dealers come to instruct.
They begin with her body
and they do not finish. They toss out sneakers
as a coda. Men move through hallways
to streets. A coat is used to cover her.
Understand this was not suicide.

Faces in windows turn
towards her body in chorus,
witness ravens untie her hair.

Skin of fish, bones of bird.

FINAL FLIGHT

The stairs of the plane are their final stadium
at Idlewild, 1961. In this black and white terminus
skaters are dressed to conquer,
arranged in a Valentine's Day send-off.
The click of the camera begins the clock:

                eight hours left.

Sabena flight #548, New York to Prague.
One stopover scheduled in Brussels.

Intimacy laces some passengers—
athletes and their parents, officials, coaches, judges—34 of the 72
know how a change of edge ruins a jump.

They know what they need to win.
They are at the top, cresting
on years of knowledge, accustomed to medals.

They can tell the difference between a clean landing
and a two-footed cheat.

Unguarded faces, gleaming eyes, laughter ringing at the flash;

lumen cut into the future.

How to register loss,
the repositories they would have become?

Each name is a world

caught in a photo, fixed
to a date by accident, a cruel lepidopterist.

Considering names, pulling them up is dangerous work.

Figures I never met
are filaments twined
into my mother's becoming,

cousin-relatives in a distant neighbourhood
accessed by dream, by passport of memory
unstamped by crisis.

One mustn't speak ill of the dead
or, I suspect, at all, of the absent.

What veneer could resist the etching of circles?

Retrace, repeat: each time
someone requests a quote on the anniversary,
grief is a scribe
lengthening the pain
rib by rib.

Before I am done looking,
she puts the photo away.

You always believe they will come back; it's just the trip is taking too long.

I count off 32 of my own teachers and companions,

enclose them in a fictional room.

Delete the room.

See what happens.

Names aboard not boldfaced:

a teen wife, a priest, businessmen, eleven of a Belgian crew.

Hit by spinning debris:

Theo, killed while tending his field (endive, chicory).
Marcel, a witness who survived but lost a leg.

Hours after impact, the calls come in waves
across time zones, words unanchored
from meaning: *they're gone, all of them gone.*
It is not a matter of thinking straight,
it is that the dial spins.
            Each hour delivers another name.

My grandfather drives to Mrs. Owen in Winchester
with his doctor's bag of sedatives to deliver the news.
Her entire family—

Those who deferred a berth
because of a broken ankle, an ultimatum from school,
or who blamed a tenth of an ordinal for keeping them home
pick through newspaper lists, searching
for details of who they will become,
                        the spaces they must fill.

Daily funeral services:
grief is a waterwheel.

Worn and grooved with pain,
she no longer answers the phone.

        Skaters return to the rink, a sudden cathedral.
        This is their ritual: prayer of movement.

In the days that follow the crash,
passersby shiver at the sight of her,
suspect they have brushed a ghost.

Fifty years later, she explains
the guilt of living,
sending her proxy to the funerals.

She cannot explain what it feels like
to have empty hands
before the families
of her friends and mentors.

Loss is not dulled by decades,
is as sharp and bright now
as their smiles at take-off.

Another photograph captures the field
outside Brussels eight hours after—

the wreckage a holy disorder.

Perhaps it was an engine, a mechanical fault, a gust
of wind or pilot error.

An answer is sighing in that Belgian field,
its ruinous connection

a linen trail of smoke.

Memory lifts a veil of ash from the glint of metal.

Only the blades remain.

SHEET

the blank sheet
pulses, begins,
pushes

the foot, line, the paragraph
measure
the body, a cycle

twist   raise   pulse.   smooth   lull   .   score

test   edge   trace

circle

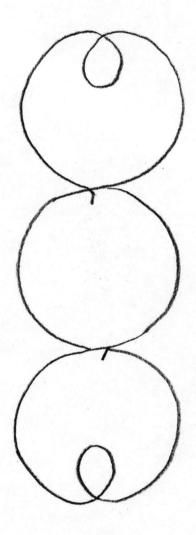

Glossary

Age-eligible
Skaters who have turned 13 but not yet 19 (21 for the man in pairs and ice dancing) before the July 1 when a new season begins are eligible to compete in Junior-level events for the whole season. Skaters who have turned 15 prior to that date in their place of birth are age-eligible for Senior-level events. The overlap in age eligibility allows for some Senior-age-eligible skaters to compete at Junior-level events, and vice versa.

Beak
Somewhat like a rocker and counter, a beak is skated on one edge without a true turn skated. A sort of shunt is skated bringing the skater to a complete stop at the apex of the figure.

Boards
The vertical barrier between the ice and the ground at the point where the ice ends. In non-Olympic competitions, boards are usually covered with advertisements for the sponsors. At the Olympics, they are usually covered by designs or the Olympic logo.

Bye
Permission to compete in an higher level of competition without having competed in the requisite qualifying competition.

Camel spin
A spin position during which the free leg is extended in the air in an arabesque position parallel to the ice.

Chack, chacked, chacking
When a medal-winning or otherwise noteworthy program is not shown on television. This term is named after Michael Chack, whose bronze-medal winning performance at the U.S. Championships was not aired on television.

Charlotte spiral
Pronounced *shar-lot*, is also known as a candle stick spiral. Named for German skater Charlotte Oelschlagel, who first performed the move in the early 1900s, it is rarely performed by men. The skater bends forward and glides on one leg with the other one lifted into the air. The skater's torso is as close to the grounded foot as possible. When performed well, the skater's legs are almost in a straight vertical split position. A charlotte can be performed either forward or backward.

Check
Stopping the rotation of a jump or a spin.

Cherry-flip
Another name for the toe-loop jump.

Cheated
A jump that was not fully rotated in midair, with either the first rotation starting on the ice or the final rotation finishing after the landing.

Code of points
An informal name for the International Skating Union Judging System.

Combination
Two or more elements (jumps, spin positions) performed in succession.

Compulsory dance
Formerly the first of the three programs in ice dance. All teams perform the same dance to standard music. In 2010, the ISU eliminated the compulsory and original dances and merged them into what is now the short dance. The compulsory portion is now officially known as the pattern dance.

Compulsory figures
Specific patterns traced in the ice by a skater's blade. While originally a major part of a skating competition, figures were removed entirely from international competition in 1990.

Counter turn
A one-foot turn on the same edge resulting in a change of lobe with the rotation outside the original lobe.

Cross stroke
In ice dancing, a step that begins with the feet crossed, the legs crossing above the knee, so the motion starts from the outside edge of the free foot.

Crossed step behind
In ice dancing, a step that begins with the free foot in the air. It is then crossed below the knee to the opposite side of the skating foot, so that the free foot touches down on the ice on the outside edge of the skating foot. The leg is crossed behind.

Crossovers
Crossing one foot over the other as a way of gaining speed and turning corners.

Crouch
A two-foot skating move in which the skater's legs are both bent at least 90 degrees.

Death spiral
An element in pair skating in which the woman skates on a deep edge with her body close to the ice and skates in a circle around the man, who is in a low pivot position and holding her by the arm.

Discipline
A part of skating governed by unique rules. Currently, the four disciplines that compete at the Olympic Games are men's singles, ladies' singles, pair skating and ice dancing.

Double
A jump with two full rotations (720 degrees) in the air (two and a half rotations for double Axel).

Draw
The act of choosing the starting order before the event. May be either open (public) or closed (private).

Edge
May refer either to part of the skate blade, or the result of skating on that part. May be either inside (towards the body) or outside (away from the body), and forward or backward, for a total of four different edges. A "deep edge" is a deep lean on the edge of the skate. Deep edges are rewarded, while skating on a "flat" (on both edges at the same time) is discouraged.

Edge jump
A general term to refer to any of the three jumps that take off from an edge.

Element
An identifiable component of a program. Includes spins, spirals, jumps, footwork, lifts, etc.

Envelope system
In the United States, the envelope system is a part of the U.S. National Team and separates skaters for The U.S. Figure Skating Athlete Support Fund (ASUPP) funding levels. Based on prescribed criteria, U.S. athletes can be placed in Team A, B, C, the reserve team or the developmental team. ASUPP financially supports the U.S. Team envelope athletes by assisting them with their skating expenses.

Exhibition
Non-competition skating or a show. Exhibitions often feature elements banned in competition as well as spotlights and show lighting. Also, the gala after a competition in which the highest-placing skaters perform a show program.

Extension
The way a body part is held in a stretched position.

Fan spiral
A spiral position in which the free leg is lifted, held upwards in front of the body, and lowered, in the style of an opening and closing Japanese fan.

Flight
A grouping of skaters at a competition who warm up together immediately prior to competing. The final flight of the free skating in single skating is made up of the highest-scoring six skaters from the short program.

Flood
Resurface the ice.

Flutz
A portmanteau of "flip" and "Lutz," for an improperly executed lutz jump, where the outside take-off edge is mistakenly changed to an inside edge, making it a flip jump.

Four Continents Figure Skating Championships
An ISU Championship for skaters from non-European countries.

Free leg
The leg that is not on the ice.

Grade of execution
A part of the ISU Judging System.

Grapevines
Figures performed on two feet.

Haircutter
A catch-foot layback spin where the free leg is brought up to head level, but not above. In some cases, the head is dropped back and it appears that the skate blade is in a position to cut the hair of the skater performing the spin. This position is often performed as a segue between a layback spin and a Biellmann spin.

Hollow
The groove in the middle of a blade between the inside and outside edges.

Hop
A small jump that does not include a rotation.

Hook
A narrow beak. Hooks, like beaks, can be skated from all edges.

Hydrant lift
A lift in which the man throws his partner over his head while skating backwards, rotates one-half turn and catches his partner facing him.

Inside edge
The edge of a skate blade facing towards the body.

I-spin
An upright spin position in which the skater pulls the free leg up in a split towards the front of the body, creating an I-position.

Jump sequence
Two or more jumps connected by turns or hops.

Kiss and cry
The area next to the rink at major competitions where the skaters wait to get their results.

Landing leg
The leg on which a skater lands a jump. Opposite of free leg. For right-handed skaters, it is usually the right leg, and vice versa.

Layback spin
A spin position in which the back is arched and head dropped back, the free leg bent behind, and the arms often stretched to the ceiling or arched overhead.

Leg wrap
An air position in jumps where the free leg is held at a right angle to the landing leg, crossing it above the knee, so that it appears to be "wrapped" around the other. Most skaters keep their legs more vertical and crossed at the ankles when they jump.

Lift
A pairs- and ice-dance element in which one skater lifts his or her partner while rotating. Pairs' lifts, unlike dance, go over the head. Some dancers perform gender-bending or "reverse" lifts, in which the woman lifts the man.

Lip
A portmanteau of "lutz" and "flip," for an improperly executed flip jump, where the inside take-off edge is mistakenly changed to an outside edge, making it a lutz jump.

Lobe
A semicircle created on the ice.

Long program (LP)
An unofficial, but widely used, name for the second and longer of the two programs performed by singles and pair skaters at a competition. The time limit is 4.5 minutes for men's singles and pairs and 4 minutes for ladies' singles at the senior (Olympic) level.

Lunge
A skating move in which one leg is bent sharply at the knee and the other is extended backwards in a straight line with the boot or blade touching the ice.

Marking the centre
To begin a school figure, the skater marks a

spot on the ice with the heel of the skate blade. This spot serves as the axis of the figure and shows the skater where to return.

Mercury scud
According to Montagu S. Monier-Williams the oldest of the hand-in-hand figures for pairs.

Mohawk turn
A two-footed turn on the same edge that continues along the same lobe.

Nationals
A country's national championships, used to decide their national champion. The highest-level competition on the national level.

Open stroke
In ice dancing, a step that is started close to the skating foot that doesn't cross in front or behind.

Ordinal
Under the 6.0 system, the skater's ranking within the group of skaters by a specific judge. Ordinals were what was counted, not the specific marks.

Over-rotated
A jump in which the skater rotates past the position for landing the jump in the air, or fails to check the rotation on landing.

Pig's ear
A rocker beak with a change, skated such that the serpentine line formed by the second curve of the beak and the change following it crosses the first curve of the beak twice.

Pivot
A two-footed movement in which one foot is flexed and the toe picks are inserted into the ice as a pivot point, and the other foot travels around the pivot point, such as the movement of a drafting compass.

Popping
During a jump, when a skater prematurely abandons their tight rotational position ("opens up") in midair, resulting in fewer than the desired rotations.

Positional jump
A jump for the purpose of displaying a position, such as stag jumps and split jumps.

Presentation
The second set of scores in the old 6.0 judging system, also known as "Artistic Impression."

Professional
Skaters who are not eligible to compete in ISU events.

Quadruple jump
A jump with four full rotations (1,440 degrees) in the air. The only quadruple jumps to have been completed in competition are the toe loop, salchow, and lutz by men, and just the salchow for ladies. In a quadruple Axel, the skater would have done 4.5 revolutions (1,620 degrees).

Rittberger
Another term for the loop jump.

Rocker turn
A one-foot turn on the same edge resulting in a change of lobe with the rotation inside the original lobe.

Roll
In ice dancing, a forward or backward edge that is either short or long. Can be a swing roll or a cross roll.

Russian split
A split jump in which the skater performs a straddle position with the legs and the body forming a V-shape. Many also touch their toes.

Sanction
Permission to hold a competition or show, granted by the ISU or national governing body. Eligible skaters may only compete in sanctioned events.

Scratch spin
An upright spin in which the skater has the free leg crossed over the ankle of the spinning leg.

Senior level
Olympic-level competition.

Sheep jump

A positional (as opposed to rotational) jump in which the skater jumps upwards and bends both legs backwards reminiscent of a sheep. The back is often arched.

Shotgun spin

An upright spin position in which the leg is held upwards towards the front of the body, but not all the way. The leg is held by the ankle or the calf, not the blade.

Shoot-the-duck

A position in which the skater travels on one foot with the skating leg bent and the other leg held forward, parallel to the ice. This is the basic position for a sit spin.

Side-by-side (SBS)

Pair-skating elements such as spins and jumps that are performed with the skaters next to each other, as opposed to pair spins or throw jumps, which are performed as a team.

Signature move

A move for which a skater is known and frequently performs, sometimes performed in a unique or unusual way.

Soldatova rule

Colloquial name of the rule stating that a skater must wait out a certain amount of time from international competition when changing the country they represent. The informal name refers to Julia Soldatova.

Spread eagle

An element performed with both feet on the ice, the blades turned out with the heels pointing towards each other. It can be performed on inside edges or outside edges.

Stag leap

A split jump in which the front leg is bent under the body.

Step-out

When a skater either under- or over-rotates a jump so that he or she does not land cleanly and must put the free leg down prematurely.

Stroking

A way of moving across the ice and gaining speed by using the edges of the blades.

Swizzle

A way of moving across the ice on two feet by pushing the feet outwards from a 90-degree-angle V and then pulling them together again, forming an oval on the ice. Also known as scissors, fishes, lemons or sculling.

Synchronized skating

A discipline of ice skating in which groups of figure skaters perform together as one unit.

'Tano jump

A jump arm position variation made famous by Brian Boitano where one arm is extended overhead instead of folded at the chest during a jump. This increases the difficulty of a jump.

Throw jump

A pair element in which one skater throws the other into the air, where she completes a normal skating jump. Throw jumps usually have more height and power than normal jumps because of the extra help involved.

Travelling

When a spinning skater moves across the ice while spinning instead of centering the spin in one spot.

Y-spiral

A spiral position in which the free leg is held up in a vertical split towards the side of the body, creating a Y-position.

Notes

"Absurd Figures" uses phrases and terms from *Figure-Skating* by Montagu S. Monier-Williams (A.D. Innes and Co., 1898), some of which are readable in the graphic sample next to the poem. It also builds on a definition of "Kitty Bar the Door," a defensive tactic in hockey. "Katy (or Katie) bar the door" means take precautions; there's trouble ahead. Further context on its political use is from "On Language: Katie Bar the Door," William Safire, *New York Times*, August 3, 2003. A phrase is borrowed from William Carlos Williams' "The Red Wheelbarrow."

"Age-eligible" is a found poem using the definition of the term.

"Aubade" comes from a line offered by Melanie Siebert to Thursdays Writing Collective as a prompt: "spring-loaded with pollen." The Purple Winecup is known to be drought-resistant, closes at night and reopens in morning. *Lisianthius nigrescens* is known as "the blackest flower." The purple Stormy Weather blooms twice a season and is disease-resistant. *Silene stenophylla* was regenerated from frozen samples 32,000 years old. An aubade is a love song in welcome, or dread, of the dawn. This poem is for angela rawlings.

"Boundary for the Married" is published in *Force Field: 77 Women Poets of British Columbia* (Mother Tongue Press, 2013).

"Circle" is for Fred Wah, built upon a line by his friend Robert Kroetsch that he brought to Thursdays Writing Collective.

"Cooling," after W. S. Merwin's *River of Bees*, repurposes some phrases and words.

"Doppelgänger" was published in *emerge* (Simon Fraser University Press, 2009) in a slightly different form and in *Harvard Medicine Magazine*, Autumn 2013.

"Final Flight" is in memory of the 34 members of the 1961 U.S. World Figure Skating Team killed en route to competition in Brussels.

"Learning to Read and Write" is for Tenley E. Albright and appears in *Event*, 40.2, 2011.

"Mercury Scud" collides seven definitions of "scud," one of which is a skating move performed hand in hand. It also appears in meteorology, explosives and war vocabulary, as a misogynous comment, and in several biological streams, including ornithology.

"Negative Patterns" was published in *Poetry Is Dead*'s sound issue, #8, Oct 2013, under the title "Don't."

"Outdoors, Ice" The words in this found poem are from two articles published in the *Harvard Crimson* in 1947, no writer attributed: "Police Search for Gardiner in River Area" and "Body of Gardiner Surfaces in Basin Sector of Charles."

"Outdoors, Water" is for Dara-Lyn Shrager.

"Rendering" is published in slightly different form in *Force Field: 77 Women Poets of British Columbia* (Mother Tongue Press, 2013). Thank you to Martha's Vineyard Museum in Edgartown, MA for their comprehensive displays on the history and mechanisms of whaling.

"School Figures" appears in slightly different form on Radarpoetry.com, January 15, 2014.

"Once a Month" appears in excerpt under a different title in *Prism International*'s 2014 Spring Issue 52:3.

"Sheet" is an erasure poem of the last page of *Marking the Centre*.

"Spiral" is written off the definition of "charlotte spiral."

"Stealing Anatomies" incorporates a list of titles from the library at the Hedgebrook Writers Retreat. The poem is written as witness to the death of Ashley Machiskinic, killed September 15, 2010 at the Regent Hotel in Vancouver. It appears in a different form in *The Writers Caravan* (Otter Press, 2011).

"Still Life" appears in *Walk Myself Home: An Anthology to End Violence Against Women* (Caitlin Press, 2011) under the title "Vancouver, Still Life" and in *Force Field: 77 BC Women Poets* (Mother Tongue Press, 2013).

"Supersedure" depends on this quote: "When a new queen is available, the workers will kill the reigning queen by 'balling' her, colloquially known as the 'cuddle death'; clustering tightly around her until she dies from overheating." *Wikipedia*, June 24, 2013. No longer active. Thank you to bee scholar Mark Winston for his notes in email correspondence in May 2015. "'Balling' is the usual term used, when the workers form a tight ball around the queen and generate heat until she dies. It's not even close to a cuddle; it's one of the more violent things that happens in the hive."

"Who You Are by What You Recognize" is a linguistic experiential map of two vocabulary streams: terms from figure skating and those that were of common use among U.S. soldiers through the period of war known as "Operation Iraqi Freedom." Terms not found in the glossary stem from military culture; some can be found on globalsecurity.org. This poem was published on LemonHound.com, issue seven, November 2013.

Glossary definitions come from USFSA.org and several pages on *Wikipedia*.

Ice pattern graphics and sampled pages from *Figure Skating* by Montagu S. Monier-Williams (A.D. Innes Co, London,1898, public domain).

Scribe drawing by Beatrice Kraljii.

Serpentine loop illustrations by the author.

Acknowledgments

A warm thank you to the mentors and friends who read various versions or contributed their energy to the development of this loop: Christie Allan-Piper, John Asfour, Lou Bernieri, Lindsay Brown, Melissa Bull, Dick Button, Wayde Compton, Jen Currin, Amber Dawn, Nick Flynn, Carolyn Forché, Joan Naviyuk Kane, Alex Leslie, Billeh Nickerson, Rachel Patterson, Rachel Rose, Dara-Lyn Shrager, Betsy Warland, Mark Winston, Daniel Zomparelli and the literary community of Simon Fraser University's Writer's Studio.

Thank you to Shortest Roommate Productions for an excellent book trailer.

Thank you to Chris Gainey for composing a musical representation of this book as "Funnel Cloud" and recording it with The University of Iowa Center for New Music Ensemble.

Thank you to the editors and journals who published poems from this manuscript and urged me on.

Thank you to the committed and fearless writers in Thursdays Writing Collective who accompany me in discovery every week and whose thoughts, comments and support are vital to my writing.

angela rawlings, whose comprehensive guidance on this experience is a brightness I am dazzled by, thank you for every part of this exchange. You barn-door opener!

Thank you, Elin Schran, playmate, for being a skilled technical advisor and editor and for choreographing this book as a skating program, which allowed me to see it as I felt it. You helped me bridge the gap between skating and writing.

Thank you to Julie Kraljii and Rhys Gardiner for shape-shifting and tender support during all the writing time.

For your potent blend of support and jubilance, for teaching us the language of movement, for raising us to befriend creativity, for reading and responding to this work with a curious mind, I love you, love you, love you, Tenley.

For the sweet encouragement, wild excitement and coziness that feed me daily, Beba, Ivar and Robert, you helped this happen in every way.

And to the wonderful Anvil Press—Brian Kaufman, Karen Green, Derek von Essen and all the staff—may every inch of care and effort you shared with this work and with me return to you 1,000 fold.